The Steam Locomotive Story

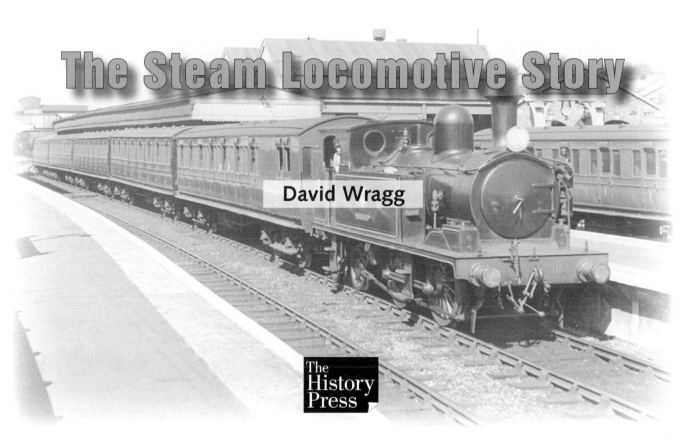

The Steam Locomotive Story

David Wragg

The History Press

Published in the United Kingdom in 2013 by
The History Press
The Mill · Brimscombe Port · Stroud · Gloucestershire · GL5 2QG

British Library Cataloguing in Publication Data
A catalogue record for this book is available from the British
Library.

Hardback ISBN 978-0-7524-8806-6

Typesetting and origination by The History Press
Printed in India
Manufacturing managed by Jellyfish Solutions Ltd

CONTENTS

nevitably in writing a book such as this, I am indebted to the National Railway Museum at York and the vast treasure trove of information contained in the NRM's search engine about the old railway companies and their locomotives. Other places where the great history of the British steam locomotive is celebrated include the Science Museum, and, of course, the many steam railway preservation societies throughout the UK and the Isle of Man.

Many of us will have heard of the 'steam age' and the 'railway age'. The two were never the same as steam first made a significant contribution to British industry by powering pumping engines for mines. There were many other industrial uses for steam, including electrical power production, and, of course, at sea. The 'railway age' is harder to quantify since it was not until steam came to be applied to the railways that the 'railway age' really began. Prior to this, there had been wagon plate tramways, and at first even on the new railways horses were often used for traction, as the load they could pull was considerably greater when on rail than on the roads. At first steam also provided the power from stationary engines to pull trains up inclines, such as that out of the London & Birmingham (later the London & North Western) Railway's terminus at Euston to Camden in London.

In fact, when the Stockton & Darlington Railway opened in 1825, it was no foregone conclusion that it would be a 'steam railway' and at first steam was reserved solely for the working of goods trains. By the time the Liverpool & Manchester Railway was nearing completion in 1829, it was clear that steam was the way forward, so the famous Rainhill Trials were held to identify the most suitable steam locomotive design ready for the opening of the line between the two cities in 1830.

Even at this early stage, the importance of the steam railway was such that the prime minister, none other than the Duke of Wellington, was present for the opening. Sadly, the new form of traction rather blotted its copybook on the day when the famous locomotive *Rocket* ran over the President of the Board of Trade, the Liverpool MP William Huskisson, who died that night from his injuries.

The power and potential of steam had been known for 2,000 years, after Hero of Alexandria had designed a rotating boiler which, when suspended above a fire, rotated as steam escaped from four nozzles. An interesting and entertaining experiment, but how to harness this discovery to a practical invention?

At around the same period in history, in both Greece and Italy grooved tracks made the movement of loaded wagons easier. In the Bronze Age in Europe, planks were laid to provide a track over which wooden sledges could be dragged more easily. Early mining was on a small scale and the markets were generally local. By the Middle Ages, in a foretaste of the Industrial Revolution, the demand for minerals and stone grew and mining and quarrying was conducted on a grander scale. The mines in the German states led the way, with shafts and horizontal galleries, and their practices spread across the rest of Europe and to the British Isles. Initially, planks were laid to improve the movement of loaded wagons or sledges with coal, but the next stage was to lay wooden rails, which not only eased movement further but also enabled larger wagons to be used, although these

➤ A.B. Clayton's painting showing the opening of the Liverpool & Manchester Railway in 1830. It was a major event that even attracted the then prime minister, the Duke of Wellington. It was the world's first railway to have double track throughout its length, although in this illustration it looks as if the locomotive is running on the wrong 'road'.

were small by modern standards and were usually able to be moved by one or two men. A centre groove was used so that a pin on the underside of the wagon would keep it on the tracks.

By the early sixteenth century, mining wagons were running on wooden planks but with flanges fitted at the inner or outer edges to give an L-shaped track, or with flanges on both sides to give a U-shape.

As mines and quarries grew in size and wagons became bigger, horses were used. In many cases, a horse would be used on the flat or to pull a wagon up an incline, while the horse would be tethered to the wagon for the descent or, in some cases, put in the wagon for a ride downhill. The horse was to remain an important feature of railway operation even after the advent of the steam locomotive, and between the two world wars horses were used in the less busy station sidings for shunting, as a

Earlier, in 1825, the Stockton & Darlington had opened as the world's first public railway, although at first steam was reserved for goods trains. This shows that the first train drew large crowds, even though it was painted some years after the event by John Dobbin.

5- or 10-ton wagon on rails could easily be handled by a horse and was cheaper and more flexible than a shunting engine. On the roads, horses drew double-deck trams before electrification. Steam locomotives for tramway work, known as 'tram engines', had a relatively short period of service and were not widely used.

By the 1600s, scientists had come to the conclusion that the power of steam could move a piston and if that could be achieved, it could in turn move a weight. In Germany, in 1650, Otto von Guericke removed the air from under a piston in a cylinder using a hand pump, and the pressure of the air above forced the piston down. A rope attached to the piston then pulled another rope attached through a system of pulleys so that a weight could be lifted.

The next step was to use steam to create the vacuum, and each puff of steam created a piston movement. The resultant steam engines were simple, but ideal for pumping and were quickly taken up for use in mines where flooding was a persistent problem.

What was recognised as the first practical steam engine was that of Thomas Newcomen, built at Dudley, Worcestershire, in 1712. This was, of course, a purely static engine.

Did you know?
After the defeat of the first bill to authorise the building of the Stockton & Darlington Railway, the preamble to the second bill made much of the value of the railway in easing road congestion by taking horses and carts hauling coal off the roads. Unusually, the mandatory use of steam locomotives was included in the bill.

Many early attempts to apply steam to locomotion were on the roads in the early nineteenth century and were doomed to failure. They were too heavy for the roads of the day and the poor surfaces made them unreliable. Greater success was found when the steam locomotive was a separate vehicle pulling the stagecoach, but most of the early attempts were for self-propelled stagecoaches. In any case, poor road surfaces still damaged the locomotive.

The design and layout of these early attempts at steam locomotion bore little resemblance to the steam locomotive as we know it today. A horizontal cylinder containing a piston was encased in a high-pressure boiler. The piston was connected to a large flywheel that drove a toothed gear, as in the case of Trevithick's first steam railway locomotive, which then drove toothed wheels on the inside of the two left-hand wheels. This was directly derived from a road steam carriage also designed by Trevithick.

◀ Richard Trevithick was one of the first pioneers, and like many of the other first-generation steam locomotive designers and builders, his early experience lay in building and maintaining pumping engines at mines, in his case tin mines in Cornwall. He had also attempted to apply steam power to stagecoaches, but with little success. This is a portrait by John Linnell.

Catch me who can.

Mechanical Power Subduing Animal Speed.

Trevithick's involvement in the steam locomotive came about almost by accident. He was installing one of his mine pumping engines at Penydarren Ironworks in South Wales, when the owner asked if a steam locomotive could be built to substitute for the horses on the 4ft 2in gauge L-shaped plate tramway that linked the ironworks with the Glamorgan Canal, almost 10 miles away at Abercynon. The locomotive when completed weighed 5 tons and hauled a load of 20 tons. The locomotive entered service in February 1804, but despite running at just 5mph, the brittle iron tramway broke several times under its weight. Its use also required much cutting back of trees and bushes so that the high chimney of the locomotive could pass through.

Trevithick built two more locomotives to this initial design, including one for the Wylam tramway in Newcastle.

It was to take more than work on isolated private tramways for the steam locomotive to catch the public imagination. Trevithick built what was described as a 'portable steam engine', named for the first time as *Catch Me Who Can*, which he took to London in July 1808. Here he set up a circular track, fenced off so that the public could be charged to view this new wonder, in what is now Euston Square. Smaller than his early locomotives, it had a horizontal boiler and a vertical cylinder, with a rod from the piston head to the rear wheels. For the first time, prints show that a small platform was provided for the driver and fireman.

Adopting the publicity slogan of 'Mechanical Power Subduing Animal Speed', *Catch Me Who Can* pulled an open carriage in which the public could ride at up to 12mph for a shilling, or stand and watch from the sides for 5d. Despite these charges, the scheme was unprofitable, and the prospects did not improve when, after a few weeks, a rail broke and the locomotive was damaged in the ensuing derailment.

Discouraged, Trevithick abandoned railways for marine engineering.

Meanwhile, in 1811, John Blenkinsop laid a rack rail line from Middleton Colliery

◀ An aerial view of Trevithick's *Catch Me Who Can* while demonstrating in London. The venue was close to the site of Euston station, because this was the first open space close to the West End and Regent's Park. It was fenced off so that spectators could enter and watch for 5d, while to ride in the carriage cost a shilling. A derailment brought the whole affair to a close within a few weeks.

A drawing showing a passenger train on the Liverpool & Manchester Railway. At the time, and for some years afterwards, carriage design owed much to stagecoach practice, but at least the open wagons have sides. It looks as if the driver is firing the engine while the fireman stands and supervises, but no doubt this is artistic licence. The four-wheel carriages would have given a poor ride.

to Leeds, and used a locomotive built to a modification of the Trevithick design. For the first time, coal and water were carried in a tender attached to the locomotive, which ran on toothed rail laid outside of the plateway thus easing the pressure on it. In June the following year, the locomotive pulled twenty-seven wagons weighing around 100 tons fully loaded over the 3½ miles between the colliery and Leeds. Four additional locomotives were built, remaining in service until 1835, while collieries on Tyneside also bought locomotives of this design.

While the rack concept reduced the risk of breaking the crude iron tramways or plateways, there was no long-term potential in the system for faster running. The use of racks, now placed centrally between the rails, has been confined to railways with steep gradients, such as the Snowdon Mountain Railway in Wales.

In 1813, back at Wylam, a step forward came when William Hedley, assisted by Timothy Hackworth, designed and built his famous *Puffing Billy* for use at the colliery. For the first time, the cylinders were placed outside the boiler, with one on each side after an earlier attempt with a single cylinder working on one side failed, and the firebox was set into the boiler with the smoke flue running to the back of the boiler and then doubled back to give the maximum heating area. This was so successful that a sister locomotive was built, *Wylam Dilly*. The one problem was that although the 5ft gauge wooden tracks at the colliery had been re-laid with iron-plate rail, this still failed under the weight of the locomotives. In 1815, to spread the weight, the frame was extended and four more wheels were added, but the extension and the extra wheels were removed in 1830 when edged rail replaced the plate; flanged

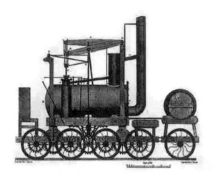

> Stephenson's famous locomotive, the *Rocket*, initially had just four wheels, but this placed too much weight on the early brittle cast-iron rails and also provided an uncomfortable ride. Its wheelbase was, therefore, extended and an extra four wheels were added. The tender at this stage was a very rudimentary afterthought.

> The caption to this illustration stated 'Old Killingworth Locomotive, still in use', but that has long since ceased to be true! Many of the early locomotives, if they survived derailment or complete mechanical failure, did manage to survive for some time. This was a colliery locomotive.

wheels were also introduced and a trailer carrying water was added.

George Stephenson initially worked as an engine-wright on the stationary engines at Killingworth, also on Tyneside, while his father worked at Wylam and had experience of the Hackworth locomotives. In 1814, he built his first steam locomotive, *Blucher*. He had seen the Blenkinsop locomotives and included many of their features, but for the first time flanged wheels were provided and edged rail was laid. Two cylinders were fitted into the boiler, and toothed wheels on the axles were connected by a chain to connecting rods linked to the pistons. The firebox was at the opposite end of the boiler from the chimney, and the crew stood on the tender. The mechanical arrangement was noisy, so the following year another locomotive was built with connecting rods driving the wheels from cylinders placed above the wheels.

Stephenson's third locomotive appeared in 1816. It was the first to use six wheels instead of four, and had axle bearings that could move freely up and down. The easier riding and improved springing led to fewer track breakages, and between twelve and sixteen were built for other mine owners, leading Stephenson to leave the colliery and set up his own locomotive works in 1823 at Newcastle, generally regarded as being the first in the world. He was to be assisted by his son, Robert, after whom the company was named.

The first steam railway to be built, as such, was the Stockton & Darlington Railway (S&DR) in the north-east of England. This was a project that emerged after consideration had been given to building a canal or tramway using horses or stationary steam locomotives. A bill to authorise the construction of the railway was rejected by Parliament in 1819, and a second bill published in 1820 was delayed by the death of King George III, so it did not receive the Royal Assent until 1821. Even this was not enough for the project to start as George Stephenson decided to change the route. A further bill had to be presented to Parliament which was enacted in 1823. It was this last measure that insisted on steam locomotives.

◄ Not all of the early railways were in the north of England, and the big exception was the Canterbury & Whitstable Railway in Kent. This is a replica of its original locomotive, *Invicta*, on display in Canterbury. Like many of the early railways, it linked a major town or city with the nearest port.

➤ A drawing of *Locomotion No.1* at Darlington, referred to in the caption as the 'No.1 Engine'. It was to be some years before photography became an important aspect of recording the development of the railways, and so much trust has to be placed in the observation skills and draughtsmanship of the railway artists.

Two locomotives were ordered from George Stephenson and both were delivered in 1825 ready for the opening of the S&DR, with two further locomotives of the same design introduced the following year. The first was eventually named *Locomotion* in 1833, and the others were also eventually named. While they were capable engines, the quality of workmanship was poor, partly because of the haphazard means of construction at the works, but also because the concept of precision engineering was in its infancy. To maintain steam pressure, drivers often adopted the dangerous practice of lashing down the safety valve, but Timothy Hackworth, who had joined George Stephenson after the father had a disagreement with his son, stopped this with the invention of the sprung safety valve.

Locomotion remained in service until 1846, and then served as a stationary pumping engine for a further eleven years. Fortunately, the North Eastern Railway (NER), which had acquired the S&DR, was amongst the first to realise the historical significance of *Locomotion* and ensured that she was preserved – a policy maintained by the London & North Eastern Railway (LNER) after the 1923 Grouping.

The next major railway was to be the Liverpool & Manchester (LMR). Again, the first bill to authorise construction was

◄ Many of the early railways used cable haulage with power by stationary steam engines. This was considered for the Stockton & Darlington, while at Euston trains needed cable haulage to reach the top of Camden Bank. This is Minories station where the London & Blackwall Railway was cable-hauled at first. Note that the machinery is completely open.

rejected in 1825, and it was not until substantial and costly changes to the route were made that a second bill was enacted the following year.

Despite the advances made by Stephenson, at this early stage there was no obvious outstanding design or builder of steam locomotives. A competition was decided upon and set for 8–14 October 1829. Known as the Rainhill Trials after the Rainhill Levels, locomotives had to run ten times in each direction over a distance

➤ One of the least satisfactory of the locomotives taking part in the Rainhill Trials of 1829 was *Novelty*, whose design was based on a simple road carriage. It was rejected when, after making just two runs, the boiler brackets gave way. It seems unlikely that this could have hauled more than a wagon or two.

➤ Also at the Rainhill Trials was Timothy Hackworth's *Sans Pareil*, which the Liverpool & Manchester Railway rejected as being too heavy at just over 4¾ tons, even though it could run at 14mph. Despite this, and a water pump failing, it was later bought by the LMR and operated until sold in 1832 to the Bolton & Leigh Railway.

of 1½ miles, with additional distance at each end for starting and stopping, then take on coal and water and repeat the performance.

The contestants varied considerably. The smallest was the *Novelty*, a four-wheeled flat truck with flanged wheels and a small vertical boiler, but this made two return runs before failing completely as the boiler joints failed. Although Hackworth's *Sans Pareil* worked well, hauling 14 tons at 14mph, it was rejected as too heavy for a four-wheel locomotive at 4.77 tons. It was a small consolation that the LMR bought the locomotive afterwards and ran it for a short time before selling it to another railway. Two more entries were rejected as they failed to attain the 10mph required by the railway.

Victory went to Stephenson's famous *Rocket*, which he built with assistance from

Did you know?

Locomotion and her three sisters did not have brakes, so had to be put into reverse in order to stop. This remained a last desperate course of action for drivers heading towards a collision or an obstruction to the very end of steam.

▲ Another early depiction of the Stockton & Darlington 'engine and car', showing the primitive wagons used both for passengers and for goods. During the early years, coke was the fuel of choice and it was some time before locomotives could burn coal efficiently. Eventually this became necessary because supplies of coke soon proved insufficient for the growing demand.

his son and from the secretary of the LMR, Henry Booth.

Rocket was a major step forward in design, having twenty-five copper fire tubes to ensure that the heat of the fire was dispersed quickly and evenly through the boiler; earlier locomotives had no more than two tubes. The firebox was behind the boiler rather than set into it, and the wheels were driven directly by two pistons, while steel springs reduced wear and tear on the track, the locomotive and the crew. The *Rocket* could be fairly designated by the wheel notation of 0-2-2.

Before the LMR opened in 1830, Stephenson produced a further locomotive, essentially an improved *Rocket*, named the *Northumbrian*, which had more boiler tubes, larger driving wheels and the cylinders set at a lower angle. It was the

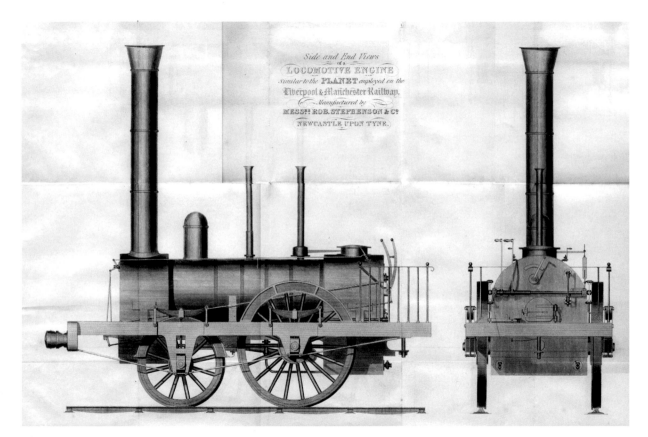

Side and End Views
of a
LOCOMOTIVE ENGINE
Similar to the PLANET employed on the
Liverpool & Manchester Railway.
Manufactured by
MESS.RS ROB. STEPHENSON & C.º
NEWCASTLE UPON TYNE.

Northumbrian that pulled the first train on the opening day. Shortly afterwards the LMR received a more refined locomotive, also by George Stephenson, the *Planet*. This was more than just a refined *Rocket*: it was the first locomotive to have a frame, at the time consisting of wood but later of iron and then steel. Also, the smokebox had a door to make cleaning the interior and the tubes easier. Another feature that influenced locomotive design for all time was the location of the cylinders at the front under the smokebox, making this the first proper 2-2-0, with the pistons driving a double-cranked driving axle.

Later locomotives often had the cylinders outside the frame, while three- and four-cylinder locomotives had them inside and outside. Variations of the *Planet* included the first locomotives designed specifically for goods traffic, with the wheels coupled together in a 0-4-0 configuration.

◀◀ The *Planet* was designed by Robert Stephenson and was one of the most significant early locomotives, with the cylinders mounted horizontally under the frame and a tender that looked suitable for the job rather than just another wagon. For the first time, the locomotive had a frame on which the boiler was mounted. The rear wheels were the driving wheels and the future single-wheeler can be seen in this design.

Did you know?

The world speed record set by *Mallard* resulted in the locomotive nearly seizing up as she was 'thrashed' by her driver and those on her footplate could smell machinery overheating. She needed major workshop attention afterwards.

The *Jenny Lind*, named after a Swedish opera star, was inspired to some extent by the Stephensons' *Patentee*, which had six wheels. Like the *Patentee* and the earlier *Planet*, it appeared on many railways, including the London, Brighton & South Coast. Designed by David Joy, locomotives of this type were soon being produced at the rate of one a week.

The shape and configuration of the steam locomotive was almost complete, but not quite. Despite the improvements, the early locomotives had been mainly four-wheeled and as a result suffered from pitching and were difficult to handle at anything but the lowest speeds. Much had still to be learnt about track and in particular the use of ballast and sleepers, which at first were often longitudinal. However, to ease some of these problems, in 1833 Stephenson designed and built a longer steam locomotive with six wheels, the *Patentee*. Only the leading and trailing wheels had flanges, but there was steam braking, and both these features were omitted by his growing number of rivals in an attempt to reproduce this locomotive without infringing his patents.

A development of the *Planet*, but almost twice as long with a 10ft wheelbase,

the *Patentee* was a 2-2-2, and the two cylinders within the frame and under the smokebox drove the two 5ft 6in main wheels. The frame was a sandwich of wood and iron for the first time. A much larger and longer boiler was possible with the new configuration, and as a result the locomotive was almost twice as heavy as the largest of its predecessors at 11½ tons. The basic design offered much scope for further experiment, and changes were made so that later variants had 0-6-0 or 0-4-2 wheel arrangements.

As the railway network grew, many of the larger companies built their own locomotive works, but there was still room for the 'independent' locomotive builder for the smaller railways and for the growing export market. British engineers and entrepreneurs started to build railways abroad, with much of the early French railway network built by British engineers. In 1837 even the Great Western (GWR), still to build its works at Swindon, bought a locomotive from Stephenson, *North Star*, a development of the *Patentee*, but built for the GWR's broad gauge. The flow of invention and innovation was not one way from George Stephenson, as from 1842 he ensured that all driving wheels on his locomotives were flanged, learning from the experience of his rivals.

◄ A portrait of George Stephenson. Like many of his contemporaries, he was both mechanical engineer and civil engineer and had come from a mine engineering background. Regarded by some as conservative, he nevertheless supported his son Robert, and when the son became the main source of new designs, the father remained as the figurehead because investors had confidence in him.

➤ Robert Stephenson, the only son of George, whose name the locomotive building company bore, even though he had only just graduated from university. His locomotive designs showed the way ahead and incorporated many features, such as horizontal cylinders, that soon became standard.

The *Patentee* was the most influential of all the early locomotives and derivatives were built as late as the early 1870s, especially on mainland Europe but also by the GWR; its chief mechanical engineer, Daniel Gooch, built more than sixty *Patentee*-type locomotives, many of them with improved cylinders that made them more economical and faster running. In 1839, Isaac Dodds invented an improved means of attaching the boiler to the frames that eliminated the stress that resulted from bolting the boiler directly on to the frames.

Boilers were also becoming more efficient. The short boilers and cramped smokeboxes of the pioneering locomotives were unsuitable for burning coal, but supplies of the fuel of choice, coke, were insufficient once demand grew with the expansion of the railways. Between 1856 and 1860, on the Midland Railway, Charles Markham conducted a number of experiments

The logical progression from locomotives such as the *Planet* and *Jenny Lind* was to the large single-wheelers such as this magnificent Great Northern Stirling 4-2-2, seen with a train of six-wheel carriages in the late nineteenth century. The single-wheelers had a long reign, and many survived to Grouping in 1923.

culminating in the extension of the firebox and improvement in the flow of air, making coal a viable fuel. At around the same time, in 1859, the French inventor Henri Gifford invented the water injector using steam to force water into the boiler even when the locomotive was standing, replacing the feed pump that could only work while the locomotive was moving. The following year, on the London & North Western Railway

> Another image of a 'Stirling Single' but on this occasion the train has six-wheel carriages at the head followed by bogie carriages. These provided greater comfort, especially as locomotive speeds increased and running at 60mph or more became possible on the main lines.

(LNWR), John Ramsbottom invented water pick-up apparatus so that a steam locomotive moving at a reasonable speed could pick up water from troughs built between the tracks without stopping.

Power was increased when Robert Stephenson invented link motion valve gear in 1841, followed in 1844 by the single eccentric drive valve gear, invented by the Belgian Egide Walschaert. In 1842,

Robert Hawthorn invented the first simple form of superheating, so that steam was reheated before being admitted to the cylinders, giving far more power. Also, without reheating free working of the pistons in the cylinders was inhibited from accumulated moisture. Locomotives without superheating thus became known as using 'saturated' steam.

George Stephenson was still improving his locomotives, lengthening the boilers to give more power. Building a large passenger locomotive in 1845, the disposition of the wheels was changed, making it a 2-2-2-0, with the driving wheels becoming those on the third axle, which had an increased diameter and were driven by two outside cylinders with the frame placed inside of the wheels. These changes were soon adopted by his competitors and the age of the large single-wheeled locomotive had arrived, although usually with the

On the London & North Western Railway, locomotives such as the *Lady of the Lake*, seen here, provided sterling service for many years as the LNWR did not treat its engines gently. In fact, a member of the class, *Waverley*, was the West Coast locomotive for the start of the railway races to Edinburgh in 1888.

middle axle in a 2-2-2 configuration being powered.

Stephenson's 2-2-2-0 locomotives with the two leading axles unpowered and the third having the driving wheels were at first rigid, but by the 1880s two-axle leading bogies took the growing weight of the locomotive and provided additional stability and reduced track wear. Later, a trailing two-wheel bogie, known as a pony truck

By the third quarter of the nineteenth century, most railways had 'singles', which included tank engines as well as express locomotives. On the Midland Railway they were known as 'Midland Spinners' because of the resemblance of the large driving wheel to a spinning wheel. This is a preserved example at a commemoration of the Rainhill Trials.

because it resembled a pony cart, was introduced under the cab.

A later refinement was to have an inside frame and a lighter outside frame. The LNWR was the main user of this type of locomotive, designed and developed at Crewe, but many other companies adopted the same pattern. Over the years, the main driving wheels became larger, eventually reaching 8ft 6in in diameter on the LNWR locomotive *Cornwall*, but diameters

Even while the singles were at their peak, compound locomotives, such as this 'latest type of North-Eastern engine', were becoming more commonplace, helped by improvements in steel technology so that connecting rods could be used. This is an M1 class of 1894. These locomotives played an important role in the railway races to Aberdeen of 1895.

Despite the compound locomotives appearing, 'Stirling Singles' were still being built, although this one had driving wheels of 7ft 6in. Unlike some of Patrick Stirling's earlier locomotives, this one had the full range of couplings and vacuum brake pipes on the front buffer bar, while previously he had been strongly opposed to double-heading.

Did you know?

With a few exceptions, mainly on narrow-gauge railways, steam locomotives needed a driver and a fireman. In 1939, the LNER fitted a 'Nu-Way' mechanical stoker to a tank engine so that it could be one-man operated, but while it worked successfully there were no further conversions, due in part to trade union resistance.

between 6ft and 8ft were much more usual. As steel tyres began to replace those of iron, starting in the 1870s, the reliability and durability of locomotive wheels improved.

Such locomotives were known as 'single-wheelers' or 'single-drivers', but there were individual company names, with those on the Midland Railway being known as 'Midland Spinners', and on the Great Northern (GNR) they were 'Stirling Singles'; the most popular type was the 'Jenny Lind', first built in 1840 by John Gray. The 'Jenny Lind' 2-2-2 had a higher-pressure boiler, inside cylinders and 6ft driving wheels. Adopted by many companies, they were especially common on the London, Brighton & South Coast, after Gray became chief mechanical engineer in 1847.

▲ The LNWR also had its single-wheelers, such as this Precedent-class *Hardwicke*, which handled the London to Aberdeen night sleeper express between Crewe and Carlisle for ten nights starting on 15/16 July 1895. The route was a difficult one with a steep climb to Shap, south of Carlisle, which was almost at sea level, and then north of the border there was the steep climb to Beattock.

▲ A contemporary engraving showing the 'Great Northern Mail' in 1894, with a travelling post office carriage immediately behind the locomotive complete with a net for catching mail bags without stopping. 'Great Northern Mail' was a description as it was not a named express.

Today, the single-wheelers seem an oddity, but their viability was enhanced with the invention of the steam sanding apparatus in 1886, which improved adhesion in slippery conditions or on steep gradients. As power and locomotive weight increased, eventually two driving wheels became more common, initially driven by separate cylinders which made starting on slippery rails difficult until steel technology became sufficiently advanced for connecting rods to be used. Nevertheless, the single-wheelers were not at such a disadvantage compared to the new compound locomotives as might be thought, as tests later showed that on a 4-4-0 locomotive the first set of driving wheels depressed the rails slightly so that the second set did not provide the tractive effort that might have been expected.

From 1882 onwards, most locomotives were built with inside framing only as the consensus amongst designers was that this was sufficient.

The question of whether cylinders should be 'inside' or 'outside' was a difficult one. Inside cylinders were protected from the full force of cold weather and so had less condensation; they were more efficient as well as giving the locomotive a cleaner profile, and were also preferred on lines with tight loading or structural gauge clearances. On the other hand, outside cylinders made maintenance much easier. When three and then four cylinders became more commonplace, locomotives had both inside and outside cylinders, and more complicated valve gear.

▲ Another engraving of the same period showing a London & North Western express passing Harrow on the main line out of Euston. The compound locomotive contrasts with the 'Stirling Single' of the 'Great Northern Mail'.

The compound locomotive was first invented in France in 1876, by Anatole Mallet. It had already been found in marine engineering with the triple expansion engine that there was still power left in the steam even as it expanded and lost pressure as it passed from one cylinder to the next. Triple expansion wasn't suitable for railways, but compounding allowed the steam to pass from one cylinder and into the next, increasing power output by up to 15 per cent. On the LNWR in 1882, F.W.

➤ A LNWR Precedent-class 2-4-0 compound locomotive, *Prince Leopold*, dating from 1877, standing at the head of an express. These locomotives also found themselves heading some of the racing trains on the West Coast route, operated jointly by the LNWR and the Caledonian Railway for journeys to and from Scotland.

➤ One of the smaller railways, the Furness Railway, served much of the Lake District and the industrial centre of Barrow-in-Furness. This venerable 2-4-0 is seen near Lake Windermere. (HMRS)

◄ On the East Coast route, trains running north of Edinburgh were handled by North British locomotives such as this M1-class (later designated M-class) 4-4-0. Although the North British lines stretched as far south as Berwick-on-Tweed, the North Eastern Railway always flatly refused to allow a locomotive change between Newcastle and Edinburgh, believing that they had the superior locomotives.

One of the many innovations that enhanced the efficiency of the steam locomotive was the water trough, which allowed water to be picked up at speed, and speed was essential if the water was to be forced up from between the lines and into the tender. This is a former Midland Railway 4-4-0 picking up water while other troughs can be seen nearer the camera. (HMRS)

◄ Another former Midland Railway locomotive under London, Midland & Scottish Railway (LMS) ownership after the Grouping of 1923. The Midland always painted the locomotive number on the tender, meaning that every locomotive needed its own tender. This was inflexible and costly as railways did not need as many tenders as locomotives since the former required much less maintenance. As can be seen, the number has been painted prominently on the side of the driving cab. (HMRS)

➤ Tender piled high with coal, this 0-8-0 was typical of the many heavy goods locomotives that most of the major railway companies operated, providing strong pulling power but not speed. Note the small wheels compared with those of express and even mixed-traffic locomotives. (HMRS)

➤➤ Usually more powerful than the humble 0-8-0 was the 2-8-0, which many companies regarded as the right configuration for a heavy goods locomotive, although the LNER liked 2-8-2 locomotives, especially for fast freight trains. (HMRS)

Webb built a 2-2-2-0 with two outside high-pressure cylinders and an inside low-pressure cylinder; an unusual arrangement because two external low-pressure cylinders could not be fitted because of restricted platform clearances. Later, four-cylinder

A former express locomotive in retirement. This was ex-Caledonian Railway No.123, clearly a 4-2-2 'single', at St Rollox Works in Glasgow, still in works grey but ready for preservation. (HMRS)

Goods locomotives seldom enjoyed the same care and attention as passenger locomotives, but this hard-working and grimy 2-8-0 was clearly a modern Stanier locomotive during the 1930s. (HMRS)

locomotives were built, starting in 1897, again with the low-pressure cylinders inside.

The more usual arrangement was for the low- and high-pressure cylinders to be adjacent whether they were inside or outside.

Superheating produced an even greater improvement in performance of up to

Locomotive classes were often decided by power classification, and this 4-4-0 GWR Class 3252, No.3287 *Mercury*, seen in 1936, had the older curved frame. (HMRS)

A GWR Class 32XX, similar in size and power to *Mercury*, was 4-4-0 No.3202 *Earl of Dudley*, with a straight frame, seen in 1935. (HMRS)

25 per cent, but the extent to which steam was superheated varied between locomotive designers. Steam simply heated in a boiler is saturated steam and contains moisture which condenses and inhibits the movement of pistons. Superheated steam

43

◄◄ Former Taff Vale
0-6-0T, while in GWR
service, sits on a turntable,
something which tank
engines were supposed
not to need as they could
run equally well in either
direction.

◄ Rack railways are a
rarity in the British Isles.
The most famous is the
Snowdon Mountain
Railway, one of whose
locomotives is seen here:
No.4, appropriately
enough named *Snowdon*.
The rack can be seen
at the bottom of the
photograph.

Now a popular
tourist attraction, the
Festiniog Railway was
originally built to move
slate from the quarries at
Blaenau Festiniog over the
13¼ miles to the harbour
at Portmadoc. It was
built to a track gauge of
1ft 11½in as the cost of
building a standard-gauge
line through difficult
country would have been
prohibitive. The double-
ended steam locomotives
are based on Robert
Fairlie's patent.

Former Southern
Railway 0-4-0ST after
renumbering by British
Railways. Such small
locomotives were useful
in shunting yards and in
railway works – this one
is in a locomotive shed at
Guildford. (HMRS)

and its moisture, instead of condensing, becomes additional steam or, if sufficient superheating is applied, it becomes a gas. Hawthorn's original superheating amounted to steam drying, while more advanced work in France in 1850 had to await improvements in metallurgy before becoming a practical proposition in the late 1890s. The

Coaling a locomotive was time-consuming and originally required much heavy labour, although coaling stages which enabled coal to be gravity-fed down into the tender from a raised platform were a step forward. With its enthusiasm for technology, the LMS introduced coaling towers in which wagons' contents were lifted to the top and dropped into bunkers or tenders. This is a 'No.1' type coaling plant in which bunkers or hoppers stored the coal until needed.

Locomotive sheds varied in design. Some were 'roundhouses' with the tracks radiating from a central turntable, while others were straight, such as this GWR example at Truro in Cornwall. Some major depots would have more than one shed, while some of the more remote sheds were very small. (HMRS)

This is the LMS 'No.2' type coaling plant in which the wagon wasn't raised, but its contents lifted by a bucket chain to fill the hoppers, and from there into the locomotive tender. The mechanised coaling plants could be worked by one man, often the locomotive fireman. They would not be used by tank engines because of the confined tender size.

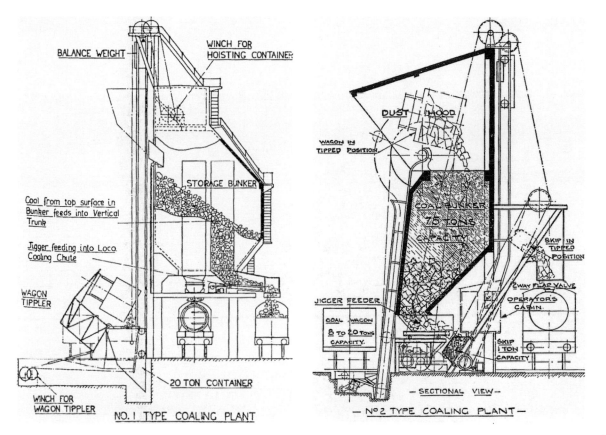

BALANCE WEIGHT

WINCH FOR
HOISTING CONTAINER

STORAGE BUNKER

Coal from top surface in
Bunker feeds into Vertical
Trunk

Jigger feeding into Loco.
Coaling Chute

WAGON
TIPPLER

WINCH FOR
WAGON TIPPLER

20 TON CONTAINER

NO. I TYPE COALING PLANT

DUST HOOD

WAGON IN
TIPPED POSITION

COAL BUNKER
75 TONS
CAPACITY

JIGGER FEEDER

COAL WAGON
8 TO 20 TONS
CAPACITY.

SKIP IN
TIPPED
POSITION

2 WAY FLAP VALVE

OPERATOR'S
CABIN.

SKIP
I TON
CAPACITY

— SECTIONAL VIEW —

— Nº 2 TYPE COALING PLANT —

49

50

◄◄ Tank engines came in all sizes and wheel notations. This was a 0-8-0T inherited by the Southern Railway from the Kent & East Sussex Railway on Grouping. Unusually for a tank engine it is named *Hecate*, doubtless a name bestowed by the previous owners. (HMRS)

◄ The end of the line on the busiest of the Isle of Wight lines: that running from Ryde to Ventnor. This is Ventnor station. The locomotive is a 0-4-4T which in Southern Railway and British Railway days bore the brunt of the island's passenger and goods services. A larger locomotive was tried, but despite being just 0-6-2T it was too big for this busy line. (HMRS)

◄◄ The Isle of Wight was another place where tank engines were always named, usually after towns and even villages on the island. This is *Ningwood*, sometimes mistakenly called *Ringwood* after a mainland town, at Ryde St Johns. (HMRS)

◄ The ability to run well in either direction meant that tank engines were not just the first choice for shunting, but also for branch lines and busy suburban commuter services, not all of which were in the London area. This GWR 2-6-2T Class 45XX is working in the Birmingham area. (HMRS)

main step forward, William Schmidt's design of 1898, was difficult to maintain, but in 1903 Jean Baptiste Flamme in Belgium devised a variation that used four steam tubes to superheat the steam and this became a system that was widely used.

The first application of the Flamme-Schmidt system on Britain's railways came in

Another GWR 2-6-2T tank with a commuter train. Turning such trains round at the terminus required considerable skill and co-ordination, with engines stopping by the water stand so that they could 'imbibe' water, and at some busy stations coaling stages were also placed conveniently. (HMRS)

Double-headed tank locomotives with a 0-6-0ST saddle tank piloting a larger 2-6-2T tank engine, possibly so that the saddle tank can be moved to where it is needed without having a light engine movement across a busy main line. (HMRS)

1906 when the GWR's George Churchward and the Lancashire & Yorkshire Railway's George Hughes introduced locomotives with superheating. The GWR had no less than 750 superheated locomotives by 1913, which saved the company 15 per cent

Water was as vital as coal to the steam railway, and perhaps even more so as a locomotive running out of coal simply stopped, while one running out of water could be badly damaged and need costly repairs. Swindon water tower provides the background to this GWR 0-6-0PT, or pannier tank, which was very much a GWR speciality. (HMRS)

In areas where the cost of building a standard-gauge railway was prohibitive, or where there were tight bends, the narrow-gauge railway was the answer and the Southern Railway bought the Lynton & Barnstaple Railway in 1922, before Grouping. This is the 2-4-2T *Yeo*. (HMRS)

Did you know?
It is important to distinguish between a locomotive and a train, as no matter how heavy, a locomotive on its own is simply a 'light engine'.

◄ Another Lynton &
Barnstaple tank engine,
Lyn. Doubtless the
cow-catcher on the front
is necessary because
of the small size of the
locomotive, which could
easily be derailed if it
struck a large animal.
(HMRS)

in fuel, even though Churchward used superheating moderately in his 4-6-0 Star class. As lubricants improved, higher levels of superheating became practical.

As the century drew to a close, 4-4-0 compound locomotives became commonplace and some companies were introducing the first 4-6-0s, although many of the early

58

◀◀ Local trains sometimes needed more than a small tank engine. This is the Southern Railway U class 2-6-0 with a down passenger train on the busy main line between Woking and Basingstoke. It is not clear how useful the diminutive smoke deflectors could be. (HMRS)

◀ Most British locomotives had the driver sitting on the left where he could see the line-side signals, but the GWR was able to place signals between its lines having originally been built for the most part to broad-gauge dimensions. The company was, therefore, the main operator of 'right-hand drive' steam engines, as can be seen here. The large lever in the centre of the picture, pointing downwards to the right, is the controller, and acted much as an accelerator would in a car. (HMRS)

59

The Southern Railway was the last to build large Pacific steam locomotives, partly because so much of its network consisted of shorter routes, but mainly because the priority for investment was electrification. Nevertheless, it did build some powerful locomotives and its Schools-class 4-4-0 was the most powerful locomotive class of this configuration in the UK. This is *Cranleigh* at speed. (HMRS)

The GWR was once home to many 4-4-0 locomotives before concentrating on 4-6-0 for express and mixed-traffic workings. This is a Class 40XX 4-6-0, *Reading Abbey*, with a parcels van immediately behind the locomotive. (HMRS)

designs with this wheel notation proved disappointing. First to introduce the 4-6-0 to Britain's railways was the Highland Railway in 1894, while the NER introduced many in 1899 and 1900, by which time the first four-cylinder locomotives had arrived in 1897.

While inevitably much attention is focused on main-line express locomotives,

Even the GWR needed heavy freight locomotives, with coal mining being a major industry in South Wales and the West Midlands, but tank locomotives were needed to bring the coal down from the valleys in South Wales before locomotives such as this Class 28XX 2-8-0 could work over the longer distances. A pannier tank is behind the tender of the 2-8-0. (HMRS)

A common scene in the days of steam was the mixed freight consisting of a variety of wagons, often headed for different destinations. The locomotive would stop to drop off or pick up wagons en route. This is a GWR Class 40 2-8-0. (HMRS)

One type of locomotive built in Britain, usually for export, was the Garratt, built by Beyer-Peacock under licence. The boiler and cab were slung between what amounted to two steam locomotives. The big advantage was heavier hauling power and greater stability, which is why so many were built for countries such as New Zealand and many African colonies with narrow-gauge main lines. This is a New Zealand example.

Both the LMS and the LNER bought Garratt locomotives in small numbers for their heavy goods trains. This is an LMS example whose performance was limited to some extent by the company insisting that it included a number of 'Midland Railway' features. (Colour-Rail)

An attempt to obtain more power from the steam locomotive led to trials with high-pressure locomotives. The LMS had a serious accident when a pipe burst on their example, but the LNER was more fortunate with No.10000, seen here whilst working the 'Flying Scotsman' express. Two crews were used, with a corridor tender so that they could change halfway through the journey between London and Edinburgh; here the two drivers and two firemen stand on the buffer bar while the chief mechanical engineer, Sir Nigel Gresley, is standing on the platform.

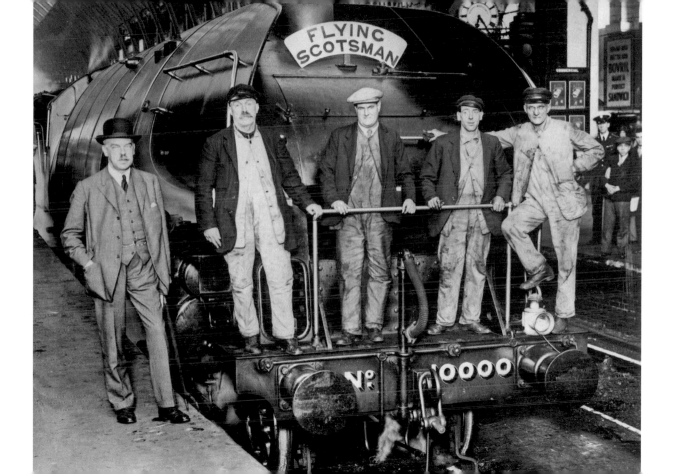

At the other end of the scale, an attempt to provide low-cost shunting locomotives to operate on poorly laid or lightweight track was provided by Sentinel, who supplied a number of their chain-driven locomotives to the LNER. Generally, they worked well, and this one clearly survived long enough to be nationalised.

Did you know?

The early diesel locomotives had poor pulling power at low speed, so the LNER tested a Kitson-Still hybrid diesel and steam locomotive, sometimes referred to as a 'steam-diesel', which switched from steam power to diesel power as the speed increased. It did this by using the opposite end of the cylinders to inject the diesel fuel. It worked well, but had to be abandoned when the manufacturer was declared bankrupt.

steady progress had been made with smaller locomotives for branch-line working and shunting. One popular configuration was the 0-6-0T, a tank engine. Tank engines had the tender integrated into the locomotive structure, usually behind the driving cab but sometimes ahead of it on one side of the boiler. There were 0-4-0 tanks, and even 2-2-2 tanks, and later tank locomotives appeared in most of the main wheel notations. The advantage

had larger tank locomotives of 2-6-4T configuration for busy suburban lines, and these could run at around 80mph.

The Metropolitan Railway, predecessor of today's Metropolitan Line, was a heavy user of tank locomotives, and even after the lines between Paddington and Liverpool Street were electrified, these continued to haul the trains on the open sections until the advent of the 1960 multiple unit rolling stock, and electrification of the entire line. For the subsurface section of the line before electrification, the locomotives were fitted with condensing gear, but steam and smoke remained a nuisance; the main benefit was the slight extension in the intervals between picking up water.

Once the compound locomotive became established, the variety of wheel arrangements increased. There was still room for the 0-4-0T on shunting duties, or sharing the same chassis or frame as a

of the tank engine was its ability to run forwards or backwards with equal ease, useful for shunting and also for branch-line working, and especially on short trips which could not afford the time for a locomotive change. The configuration meant that tank engines were only suitable for short journeys because of the limited amount of coal and water that could be carried, and water pick-up apparatus was found to be unsuitable as the inflow of water at speed could burst the tanks. Many railways

◄ While there were a few one-man-operated steam locomotives, mainly on narrow-gauge lines or in sidings or works railways, most were operated by a driver and fireman. This locomotive was modified to use the 'Nu-Way' mechanical coaling system, with two spirals moving the coal from the tender to the firebox. This worked successfully, but union objections ensured that there was only one conversion.

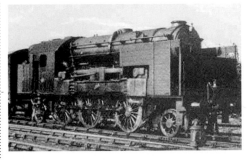

➤ The early diesel shunters suffered from low power at low speed, and in an attempt to address this the LNER conducted trials with the Kitson-Still steam-diesel.

carriage so the locomotive and carriage were combined into a 'railmotor'. Some of the later LNER railmotors had the locomotive hidden within the coach work, so that unless working hard or letting off steam, the casual observer might have believed them to be diesel railcars. At the other extreme were the Garratt articulated locomotives of 2-8-8-2 configuration, with two sets of driving wheels; however, while common in many countries, including those of southern Africa, they were only to be seen in small numbers on Britain's railways serving with both the LMS and LNER.

There were distinctions between companies. The Midland Railway had many tight bends on its routes and so favoured small locomotives of 4-4-0 configuration; as train lengths and weights increased, double-heading became commonplace. On the steam railway, double-heading meant twice as many footplate crew, unlike electric and diesel traction which could have almost any number of locomotives or self-propelled multiple units with a single driver. Apart from its freight 2-8-0s, even the mighty Great Western tended to favour nothing heavier or larger than 4-6-0, but the company's King class, powerful as it was, was restricted in the number of routes it could work. The paradox was that it was the GWR that had Britain's first 4-6-2 or Pacific locomotive, *The Great Bear*, but while a source of pride to the directors, it was a one-off and a nuisance, so it was later rebuilt as a King and renamed. There was another paradox in that the small locomotives of the Midland were joined by one of the most powerful locomotives on Britain's railways, the 0-10-0 or 'decapod'. Unique not only on the Midland Railway but also in the country, it was used as the banker boosting heavy trains ascending the steep Lickey incline.

The Southern Railway needed Pacific locomotives, but for many years had to make do with 4-4-0 and 4-6-0 configurations, although the 4-4-0 Schools class was the most powerful locomotive of its type in the UK. For the Southern, investment went into electrification, and it was not until the Second World War that the new chief mechanical engineer, Oliver Bulleid, was able to introduce his Merchant Navy-class Pacifics and their smaller cousins, the West Country and Battle of Britain classes. These had many unusual features and, while brilliant locomotives when all was going well, could also be troublesome and prone to major failures.

The true homes for the Pacific were the LNER and the LMS. However, operations were hampered by the LMS inheriting the Midland's vast stock of small locomotives, and the company suffered delays in obtaining powerful Pacific locomotives until after Stanier became chief mechanical engineer. Opposed to the mighty Pacific locomotive was the operating department of the LMS because, while there was no question that the power was needed, widespread introduction of Pacifics meant that many turntables would have to be replaced, a major cost at a time when the economy was in recession. As a result, the LMS was forced to build 4-6-0s based on the Southern Railway's Lord Nelson class, which became the Royal Scot class and was first seen on the express of that name.

It was not until Sir William Stanier was wooed away from the GWR to become chief mechanical engineer of the LMS that the company started to get the Pacific locomotives that it needed. First of all was the Princess Royal class, first seen in 1933, but these were to be eclipsed by the Coronation class. The first examples were heavily streamlined, although this was later removed to ease maintenance and reduce weight, producing a very impressive and handsome locomotive.

Meanwhile, the LNER started life with a stud of Pacific locomotives which it soon enlarged. For the best part of two decades, the most famous of these were the A1-class Pacifics such as the *Flying Scotsman*, all but one of which were later rebuilt as A3s. The real stars were the A4 class, which started to appear in 1937, initially on the 'Silver Jubilee' express between London King's Cross and Newcastle.

In 1938, one A4, *Mallard*, set a speed record of 126mph, which has never been beaten since by a steam locomotive anywhere in the world. The A4s all retained their streamlining up to the end of their service.

One of the most successful locomotives of the inter-war period was Stanier's Class 5 mixed-traffic locomotive, a 4-6-0 known affectionately as the 'Black Five', first seen in 1934. Like the Princess Royal class, the 'Black Five' owed much to Stanier's GWR experience. The following year he produced a freight development with a 2-8-0 wheel configuration, which many of the railway companies found to be the most suitable arrangement for heavy goods locomotives.

The LMS also developed a tank engine with 2-6-4T wheel arrangement for heavy commuting duties, especially around London and Glasgow.

While the LNER also had 2-8-0 locomotives, many pre-dating Grouping, Sir Nigel Gresley introduced his V2 2-6-2 mixed-traffic locomotive in 1936, of which many were taken up by the War Office during the Second World War. Unlike the 'Black Fives', the first batch was painted in LNER green, largely to publicise the new 'Green Arrow' express goods service, and unusually for mixed-traffic locomotives the first eight were named, with the first being *Green Arrow*.

The need for more power caused designers to pursue many different avenues. One method attempted by the LNER was to fit boosters to the trailing wheels of the 4-4-2 Atlantics, with a cylinder and piston working on the pony truck. This attempt at a short cut failed as without additional boiler capacity there was little benefit gained.

Between the wars, much hope was placed in higher-pressure boilers to ensure

a viable longer-term future for the steam locomotive, which many still saw as the advanced technology of the day, especially on the LMS and LNER. The LMS prototype *Fury* suffered a spectacular failure when a steam pipe burst during trials, leaving one man dead and another seriously injured. The LNER locomotive, simply numbered 10000, also served as an early experiment in streamlining. While it did not suffer any serious accidents or incidents, it was unpopular with the maintenance teams as it needed constant attention.

While the original railways had varied track gauges – most inconveniently on the Great Western which had a 7ft broad gauge, meaning that goods had to be transhipped at stations such as Gloucester where broad gauge and standard gauge met – gauge standardisation was soon enforced. The GWR was not the only culprit as the Great Eastern for many years had a 5ft gauge. Ireland had a different gauge, at 5ft 3in.

Despite this, standard gauge, of 4ft 8½in, was too wide and too costly to lay in many remote areas, especially where difficult terrain meant there had to be tight curves. In Wales, several narrow-gauge railways were built, including the Festiniog at 1ft 11½in, originally to handle slate traffic. In Ireland, there were complete systems, such as the County Donegal and the Londonderry & Lough Swilly, at 3ft gauge, which were necessary because of the high cost of building at 5ft 3in. The soft terrain in parts of Kent meant that, unusually, a passenger narrow-gauge railway was built in 1927, the Romney Hythe & Dymchurch Railway, with a gauge of just 15in. Strangely, this used locomotives designed as miniatures of both British and American main-line steam engines.

A succession of great locomotive engineers propelled the steam railway to ever greater triumphs. Many of these men were heroes of the day, with honours bestowed upon them. Each generation had their man, or perhaps men, driving the steam railway forward. Many people have their favourites, but who were the 'greatest' is a difficult question. It is hard to compare the work of George Stephenson with that of Gresley with almost a century between them. Stephenson will always be famous for his *Rocket*, but Gresley's lasting memorial is *Mallard*, the fastest steam locomotive in the world.

◄ Patrick Stirling was the chief mechanical engineer for the Great Northern Railway at the time of the railway races between the East Coast and West Coast companies in 1888 and 1895. He was famous for his 'Stirling Singles' and opposed double-heading.

It is clear that George Stephenson has to be one of the great engineers. As engineer to the Stockton & Darlington Railway, the former colliery engine-wright had a number of inventions to his credit, which he brought together in the *Rocket*. His work on the Liverpool & Manchester Railway included crossing the marshlands of Chat Moss. He followed this by becoming engineer for a number of railways. Despite

◄ Sir William Stanier joined the LMS from the GWR, and despite his background immediately started to build the Pacific locomotives that his new company so desperately needed, starting with the Princess Royal class. Perhaps his most famous locomotive was his Class 5, or 'Black Five', 4-6-0.

► Sir Nigel Gresley with *Sir Nigel Gresley*. The LNER had a reputation for being 'poor, but honest' and one perk was that the senior officers had locomotives named after them. The A4 was Sir Nigel's crowning achievement, setting a world speed record for steam that remains unbeaten, but perhaps his most significant class was the V2 mixed-traffic locomotive.

◄ The man who set the pattern for GWR locomotives was George Churchward, whose Star class in particular led the way to first the Castle class and then the King class, both of which were designed by his successor Collett, who seemed at times to be reluctant to make too many changes. He built Britain's first Pacific locomotive, but this was later converted to a Castle. (National Railway Museum - NRM)

> Oliver Bulleid was the last chief mechanical engineer for the Southern Railway. He provided the Pacific locomotives that the company needed for its heavy boat trains, Pullmans and West Country expresses. Instead of streamlining he used air-smoothed casing that led to the Merchant Navy class and the smaller West Country and Battle of Britain classes being known as 'Spam Cans'. He persuaded the authorities that these were really mixed-traffic locomotives, as express locomotives could not be built during the Second World War. (NRM)

An official Southern Railway press photograph of the first Merchant Navy-class locomotive. These were all named after major shipping lines, and as the Southern Railway was the largest operator of ferries across the English Channel, what better name than *Channel Packet* for the locomotive? (Southern Railway)

While every other railway was planning to build Pacifics, or in the case of the Southern the operating department was demanding them, the GWR, which had built Britain's first Pacific, converted it to a Castle-class 4-6-0 in 1924. Unusually, in its new guise the former *Great Bear* became *Viscount Churchill*, after the GWR's chairman at the time. (HMRS)

Rather than build Pacifics, the GWR built the King class, still a 4-6-0 but far more powerful; unfortunately it was also very heavy so the axle weight restricted the number of routes on which it could be used. Looking splendid while still new from the workshops in April 1939 is *King George VI*, in shining contrast to the years of austerity that were to follow. (HMRS)

◀ The Great Western King class were the company's most powerful locomotives, although because of their high axle weights they were not available on all lines. This is *King Edward I* in preservation at Didcot. (Tony Higgert)

➤ Much humbler, and much earlier, this 1930 shot of a Grange class still shows the care with which a GWR locomotive could be presented. It could take two teams of up to eight men several hours to clean and prepare a steam locomotive for service. The process of building a fire to heat the water could take several hours, with the fireman on duty an hour before the locomotive was needed to ensure that the right steam pressure was reached. (HMRS)

▲ This was a GWR Hall class mixed-traffic locomotive, also
known as a Class 49XX. This is *St Bride's Hall* outside Swindon
works. She has a larger tender than usual for this class. (HMRS)

◄ Wartime prevented the Southern Railway from electrifying the busy line from London to Southampton and Bournemouth, while it enabled Bulleid finally to introduce Pacific locomotives by arguing that they were really mixed-traffic rather than express engines. Here, Merchant Navy-class No.35017, *Belgian Marine*, arrives at Waterloo with the 'Bournemouth Belle' all-Pullman train, while in the background is an electric train bound for the other Hampshire port, Portsmouth. (HMRS)

◄ The Second World War found the Southern Railway at a major disadvantage with rolling stock generally more suitable for passenger operations than freight. An urgent programme of construction led to the provision of forty utility locomotives known as the Q1 class. Designed by Bulleid, many of his features can be seen. This is the sole preserved Q1 seen at Sheffield Park on the Bluebell Railway in Sussex. (Oxyman/ Wikipedia)

his achievements, many historians regard him as being ultra-conservative, but he did give others, including his son Robert, their head, and created forward-thinking teams. However, it was George Stephenson's name and reputation that attracted investors.

Skipping a couple of decades, we come to Patrick Stirling. Having worked with marine engines and locomotive builders, he became locomotive superintendent of the Glasgow & South Western Railway in 1853 before moving to the GNR in 1866, where he was soon promoted to chief locomotive superintendent. At the GNR he introduced a series of locomotives, including the first of his famous 'Stirling

➤ Seen shortly before withdrawal in the late 1960s, this is Stanier's idea of what a heavy goods locomotive should be: his 2-8-0 8F class. This was used as the standard goods locomotive design for all railways during the Second World War. Seen in British Railways' days, the dirty appearance would have been typical of many locomotives during the war years due to hard work and limited manpower.

Singles' in 1868, although the most successful of these was the 4-2-2 with an 8ft driving wheel, first seen in 1870. He objected to double-heading, so at first he built locomotives without steam pipe connections on the front buffer bar, and disliked coupled locomotives and bogie passenger stock.

George Churchward came from farming stock but started his railway career on the South Devon Railway before moving to the GWR and working under William Dean. He rose to carriage works manager at Swindon in 1885, and then locomotive works manager, eventually becoming chief mechanical engineer in 1902. In

Seen with a passenger train, the LNER's V2 class were so highly regarded that the War Department ordered many of these 2 6 2 locomotives for use by the British Army, especially overseas. No.60975 is seen here after nationalisation at Newstead

his new role he was responsible for the standardisation of locomotives, with nine standard types which were augmented by further standardisation of components. He also created the typical 'GWR look', with his locomotives having tapered boilers and long-travel valve gear. His four-cylinder locomotives adopted the divided drive found on French locomotives imported by the GWR, and he was one of the British pioneers of superheating.

Under Churchward, Swindon works was remodelled and Europe's first locomotive testing plant built. He introduced the first 70ft passenger carriages and, in 1908, built Britain's first Pacific locomotive, *The*

Did you know?

In 1903, Britain's railways adopted a standard wheel notation for their locomotives. This was named 'Whyte's Notation' after its inventor, F.M. Whyte. The notation 4-6-2 meant that the locomotive had four unpowered wheels on bogies, six powered driving wheels and two wheels on small trailing bogies, usually known as a pony truck. The notation was read left to right, with the left being the front of the locomotive and the right being the driving cab.

Some of the more common wheel arrangements had names:

4-6-2 was a 'Pacific'

4-4-2 was an 'Atlantic'

4-6-4 was a 'Baltic'

2-6-0 was a 'Mogul'

2-8-2 was a 'Mikado'

The same notation was used for tank engines, with a 'T' suffix, and 'PT' meant a pannier tank and 'ST' a saddle tank.

◀◀ Lighter than the Merchant Navy class was the West Country class, here running into Kent and about as far as it could get from the West Country. This is *Torrington*. (HMRS)

> ➤➤ Bulleid might have cheated with his three classes of 'Spam Cans', but there could be no doubting the utilitarian credentials of the wartime Q1 class. Nevertheless, there are still a number of visual clues that suggest a relationship with his other locomotives. This was a goods engine without question. (HMRS)

Great Bear. His Star-class 4-6-0 express locomotives influenced all subsequent GWR locomotive design.

Charles Collett also had early experience in marine engineering, before joining the GWR in 1893. He followed Churchward as chief mechanical engineer in 1922, and continued his work developing a largely standardised locomotive fleet. His Castle class was a development of Churchward's Star class, while the Hall-class and Grange-class two-cylinder mixed-traffic locomotives were derived from the earlier Saint class. His most notable locomotives were the King class, built between 1927 and 1930, and were the heaviest and most powerful 4-6-0 locomotives in Britain. On the ground he further improved the GWR's workshops and engine erection methods, with greater precision leading to greater durability. He also extended automatic train control (ATC) to all the GWR's main routes.

Having trained with the LNWR at Crewe and then worked for the Lancashire & Yorkshire Railway, before becoming carriage and wagon superintendent and eventually chief mechanical engineer of the GNR, Nigel Gresley (later Sir Nigel, after being knighted in 1936) was in just the right position to become chief mechanical engineer of the LNER on its formation in 1923. The LNER was heavily decentralised in its management structure, making Gresley one of a very small team of 'all line' officers. He was a proponent of articulation for passenger rolling stock, using this both to increase capacity within the overall train length and improve riding on six-wheel suburban stock, and later to improve riding and reduce the weight of express stock. Examples of his work include four-carriage suburban stocks, or 'quad-arts', and three- and five-carriage express rolling stock, including a five-car dining set.

89

He introduced electric cooking equipment for dining cars in 1926, and in 1930 he introduced pressure ventilation on express passenger stock, following this with air conditioning.

He improved the performance of steam locomotives with conjugated valve gear and many of his locomotives were highly successful, including the V2 2-6-2 mixed-traffic locomotives. But he is most famous for his A4 Pacifics with one, *Mallard*, setting a world speed record for steam of 126mph in 1938.

A contemporary of Gresley and a rival, William Stanier (later Sir William, after being knighted in 1943) was apprenticed on the GWR under William Dean, and rose to become principal assistant to Collett. He moved to the LMS at a time when the company desperately needed larger and more powerful locomotives. He incorporated many GWR features into his designs, such as tapered boilers, but also used outside Walschaert's valve gear for ease of maintenance. He is best known for his outstanding Class 5 4-6-0 'Black Five' mixed-traffic locomotives and his 2-8-0 freight locomotives.

Gresley's assistant at the GNR and then the LNER was Oliver Bulleid, who left to join the Southern Railway in 1937, at a time when the company's need for powerful steam locomotives had been neglected in the pursuit of electrification. Despite the Ministry of War Transport insisting that only goods and mixed-traffic locomotives could be built, using a standard design, he managed to produce his 'Spam Cans' – the air-smoothed Merchant Navy, West Country and Battle of Britain classes, all 4-6-2s – by arguing that they were mixed-traffic locomotives. While these had many advanced features, the totally enclosed chain-driven valve gear was prone to major failures, and when they were rebuilt after nationalisation, a more conventional valve gear was chosen. Bulleid also built the Q1 utility locomotive. His Leader class, in effect a double-tank engine with the appearance of an electric or diesel locomotive with cabs at each end and officially a C-C notation rather than 0-6-6-0, was impractical as the heat in the fireman's compartment was unbearable. He did, however, design a prototype 1,750hp diesel-electric locomotive that provided the basis for 350 built by British Railways with increased power.

The approach of the pre-1923 railway companies to higher speeds varied. The LNWR believed that 40mph was sufficient, and that higher speeds meant increased coal and water consumption as well as putting extra pressure on the track. This approach was challenged by the company's involvement in the railway races to Edinburgh of 1888 and to Aberdeen of 1895, in each case between the East Coast and West Coast companies. It took two companies to maintain the services on each route until 1895, when the race through to Aberdeen required three companies to collaborate on the East Coast route.

The irony was that while significant gains were made in higher speeds and much reduced through-journey times, afterwards the East and West Coast companies opted for an eight-and-a-half-hour through day-journey time between London and Edinburgh or Glasgow. The agreement survived Grouping in 1923, even when the *Flying Scotsman* started non-stop running, so that the train following making four stops took the same time! Eventually, the night sleepers took less time than the day expresses.

The LNWR's parsimony is better understood in the context that the travelling public still had the choice of coastal liner services, and these were much cheaper than railway travel, especially for those prepared to travel as deck passengers. If the journey involved changing from train to ship or vice versa, and perhaps then changing back again, as one would travelling from, say, London to Derry, taking a coastal liner could be the most direct and attractive option, even though not the fastest or most frequent.

True, high-speed running and the desire to set speed records only arose when there was competition, as between London and Scotland, or, largely forgotten because of changes over the years, for the transatlantic boat train traffic between Plymouth and

Did you know?

Picking up water while on the move was a time-saving but highly risky business. It was left to the locomotive fireman to keep a look out for the sign warning of the approaching water trough so that the scoop could be lowered and the maximum volume of water lifted. It was even more important to see the sign warning that the scoop should be raised, otherwise a derailment could occur. The locomotive had to be moving at a reasonable speed otherwise the scoop would not be moving fast enough for water to be forced up and into the tender. At Grouping in 1923, only the Southern Railway did not use water troughs.

94

◀ Despite the quick work in putting the name of British Railways on the tender, Lord Nelson-class 4-6-0 *Lord Anson* looks none too well cared for as she imbibes from a water column at Basingstoke. (HMRS)

◀ One of the powerful yet compact Schools-class locomotives on a Waterloo–Plymouth express, seen at Salisbury. She may have been taking on water as the Southern was alone in not having water troughs and the range of a Southern express locomotive without taking on water was around 80–100 miles. (HMRS)

Ironically, Bulleid's Merchant Navy class were too heavy to take the weighty boat trains into Southampton Docks, a duty for which the scaled-down and lighter-weight Battle of Britain and West Country classes were used. This is a preserved Battle of Britain-class Tangmere on a trip for enthusiasts at Salisbury. (geograph.org via Wikipedia)

The Southern was not the only company to have to wait for its Pacific locomotives, and while the LMS was ahead, it too had to rely on 4-6-0 locomotives at first. The Royal Scot class was nevertheless so highly regarded that the first locomotive after which the class was named was sent on a tour of the United States. She is seen here after her return, without the cattle-catcher with which she had been fitted to comply with US railway regulations, but still with a US-style bell. She also seems to have the headboard for the 'Royal Scot' express. (HMRS)

London, which saw the GWR and the London & South Western companies vying for traffic.

It was this traffic that was behind the *City of Truro* setting an unofficial record of more than 100mph in 1904. This record was disputed over the years, but recent research has concluded that the claimed speed was in fact achieved and the locomotive may have reached 102.3mph. That same year, the GWR introduced a seven-hour through schedule for the 312 miles between London and Penzance, and soon discovered that traffic grew with improved speeds.

The GWR by this time had long converted from broad gauge to standard

When the LMS did finally get its Pacific locomotives, it was in the form of Stanier's Princess Royal class. One of these, *Princess Elizabeth*, set new records on a return run between London and Glasgow. She is seen here in the workshops. (HMRS)

◀ Completely unmistakeable were the Coronation-class locomotives that followed, with their extensive streamlining and their own livery – initially blue with white stripes that continued along the carriages, and then later red with gold stripes, far more suited to the LMS corporate identity. This is *Princess Alice*. One of these locomotives set a speed record of 114mph in 1937. The most powerful locomotives in Britain, some believe they could have gone faster than the LNER's *Mallard*, but this never happened. (HMRS)

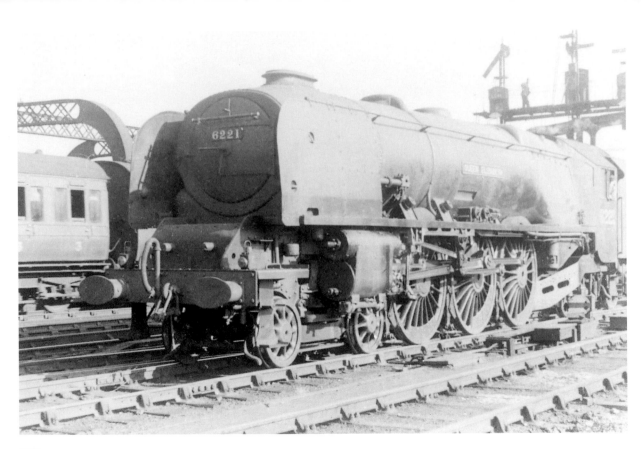

◄◄ Later Coronation-class locomotives, usually known as the Duchess class, dispensed with the streamlining which added weight and made maintenance more time-consuming, while the original locomotives also had their streamlining removed. This is *Queen Elizabeth*, without her streamlining, and many believe that a much more impressive locomotive resulted. (HMRS)

◄ The A4s kept their streamlining from the day they were built to the day they were retired. Most famous was, of course, *Mallard*. She is seen here on the post-nationalisation locomotive exchanges, with 'British Railways' no doubt quickly added to her tender.

gauge, but it is interesting that at no time when using broad gauge did the company attempt speed records, even though it should have been possible for broad-gauge locomotives to run faster than those on standard gauge, largely because the broad-gauge track would have had fewer tight curves.

Speed records not only include the special attempts, often with trains that are 'short-formed' – having fewer carriages than usual, as in the races of 1888 and 1895 – but also regular scheduled passenger workings, which is when the commercial advantage is most likely to arise.

In 1923, the GWR introduced the train unofficially but popularly known as the 'Cheltenham Flyer', between Cheltenham and London Paddington. This was the fastest express in Britain and after several

◄ The plaque on the side of *Mallard* that proudly says it all.

LNER

ON 3RD JULY 1938 THIS LOCOMOTIVE ATTAINED A WORLD SPEED RECORD FOR STEAM TRACTION OF 126 MILES PER HOUR

➤ No doubt many were disappointed that No.10000 never set a record. Her one claim to fame was that she was known in the press as the 'hush-hush locomotive', with journalists maintaining that it was because she was quieter than other steam locomotives. In fact, the 'hush' referred to the secrecy with which she was built! Here she is crossing the Forth Bridge.

accelerations, eventually offered the world's first 70mph timings, but only between Swindon and Paddington. On one occasion, a record of 81.6mph was set.

It was not until the 1930s that the LMS and LNER started to improve timings between London and the two main Scottish cities. Even when non-stop running started between London and Newcastle in 1927, the average speed was just 48.7mph, less than achieved on the races to Aberdeen, but the Newcastle service consisted of full trains.

In November 1936, the LMS Princess Royal-class *Princess Elizabeth* ran from Glasgow Central to London Euston at an average speed of 70mph, despite the lack of streamlining, with a load of eight carriages and in high winds and driving rain. The following year, the new streamlined locomotive *Coronation*, with eight carriages, set a record of 114mph between Stafford and Crewe. Despite this achievement, when the 'Coronation Scot' express was introduced between London Euston and Glasgow, full use was not made of the powerful locomotives and the through-journey time was six and a half hours, when

◄ Built to handle heavy expresses over the difficult line between Edinburgh and Aberdeen, *Cock o' the North* was a 2-10-2 Mikado, or in LNER terms, P2. She had a similar styling to No.10000, but others had A4 styling. They were not a great success as their heavy weight and long wheelbase meant that there were few other routes which they could work when not needed for the Edinburgh–Aberdeen services.

A view into the driving cab from the tender. The interesting feature is the canvas surrounding the top of the cab, which suggests that it was a wartime view: the canvas would be draped between the cab and tender so that enemy aircraft could not see the flames from the fire. (HMRS)

many believe that six and a quarter hours or even six hours would have been possible.

In July 1938, the LNER gave its response to the LMS record when the A4 locomotive *Mallard* reached a world record speed of 126mph with seven carriages. She was chosen for the record attempt because she was one of just three A4s to have the Kylchap exhaust arrangements with a double blast-pipe and chimney.

The double blast-pipe and chimney was one of a number of improvements made by the French locomotive engineer Andre Chapelon. Starting in 1929, he showed how eliminating pressure losses in constricted and complicated steam-pipe arrangements, with steam chests of inadequate volume, could improve the efficiency of existing locomotives by as much as 40 per cent.

The late 1930s, the eve of the Second World War, showed the steam locomotive at its peak of efficiency and glamour.

Did you know?
The range of a large express locomotive without picking up water either from troughs or imbibing at a stop was around 80–100 miles.

Tenders varied in both coal and water capacity, but water was the more usual limitation on how far a locomotive could work, as the LNER had tenders that could carry sufficient coal, usually around 7 tons, for the non-stop run from London to Edinburgh.

A steam locomotive that could consume 15lb of coal per mile was regarded as economical. An express running at high speeds with a heavy train would consume at least twice as much.

The war years that followed were to see speeds reduced and utilitarian construction, although there were also attempts to simplify locomotives to make maintenance easier and less expensive, and to ensure that optimum performance was delivered consistently.

The new classes of locomotives were generally designed to operate across the individual company networks on any routes or trains that required the available power. There were exceptions, of course, in the hunt for ever more powerful locomotives. On the Southern, the irony was that Bulleid's Merchant Navy class, named after the leading shipping lines of the day, were too heavy to enter Southampton Docks, so the boat trains were hauled by Battle of Britain- or West Country-class locomotives which looked like scaled-down Merchant Navy-class locomotives; collectively all three classes were known as 'Spam Cans' because of their square, air-smoothed shape. On the GWR, Collett's King class was far too heavy for many routes, including the busy trains to the Cornish Riviera.

It was also the case that exceptions had to be made to satisfy particular demand. The Beyer-Garratt articulated locomotives obtained in small numbers by the LMS and LNER were an example of this as an attempt to improve the working of heavy freight trains.

On the LNER, the difficult line from Edinburgh to Aberdeen often required the double-heading of heavy passenger expresses, and in an attempt to ensure that just a single locomotive took over on arrival at Edinburgh Waverley from the south, a new class, the 2-8-2 Class P2 or Mikado, was introduced, with the first being named *Cock o' the North*, which entered service in May 1934. The largest and most powerful British express locomotive of the day, it used

◄◄ Locomotives were often modified during their working lives, and this ex-Southern Railway King Arthur class, *Joyous Gard*, seen after nationalisation, was fitted with multiple jet blast-pipes and a large-diameter chimney. (HMRS)

the same cladding first seen on No.10000. For the first time, a British steam locomotive was sent to the testing station at Vitry-sur-Seine in France. Of the six P2s built, the final four used A4-style streamlining. The trouble was that magnificent though they appeared, these locomotives showed no real economy when working over the line between Edinburgh and Aberdeen, and their weight made them difficult to allocate to other routes when there was insufficient need for them on the Aberdeen expresses.

Many of the chief mechanical engineers of the early railway companies had worked towards standardisation, starting with Churchward on the GWR who not only standardised locomotive classes but also components, eventually providing 1,100 standard items. Nevertheless, the individual companies prior to 1923 had their own preferences and policies, often driven by their own circumstances. The Midland Railway favoured small locomotives while the LNWR was averse to speed. Even such items as controls differed between companies. A few companies had the driver sitting on the right-hand side of the cab, while most had him on the left so that he could see the signals. The largest of the 'right-hand drive' companies was the GWR, a legacy from the broad-gauge days that meant that once the conversion to standard gauge was completed, there was room between the lines for signals to be placed.

The big priority on Grouping in 1923 was to reduce the number of different locomotive classes, and to standardise as many components as possible.

Much standardisation was achieved by a policy of 'scrap and build', which was expensive, especially at a time when the economy was suffering from the impact of the Great Depression. The GWR undertook some substantial rebuilding of inherited locomotives, but also had to scrap many. Of all the railway companies that passed under its control in 1923, the Taff Vale was the one that had most of its locomotives retained, largely because many had, in fact, been built by the GWR.

The GWR and the LMS were the leaders in standardisation. It had long been a

◄ It took some time for a new British Railways corporate livery to be agreed and implemented, so at first locomotives were renumbered and the name British Railways was painted over their old company titles, as with Battle of Britain-class *615 Squadron*, still in SR livery. (HMRS)

▲ Despite looming nationalisation, the railway companies continued behaving, up to the very last minute, as if nothing was going to change. This dapper GWR 0-6-0, therefore, was outshopped in 1946 in full livery. (HMRS)

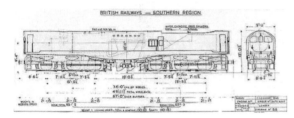

In an attempt to produce a powerful steam locomotive with the flexibility of a diesel or, in the Southern's case, electric engine, Bulleid designed his Leader class, effectively a 0-6-6-0 tank, or perhaps even a C-C. However, while the driver had a good view, the fireman's position was so hot as to be unbearable.

The end driving cabs and the fireman's position, about a third from the right, can be seen in this plan drawing.

policy for the GWR, and under Stanier this approach spread. He did not go so far as to place a maximum size of 4-6-0 configuration on his locomotives, but there were distinct features common to his main classes of locomotive – such as the tapered boilers and the design of the driving cabs – that gave

On the other hand, the GWR locomotive *County of Somerset*, seen here in 1947, looked just about ready for a new coat of paint. (HMRS)

Did you know?
The former LNWR and Midland steam locomotives had regulators that worked in the opposite directions. The Midland practice was the standard for most railways, and when an ex-Midland driver found himself in a former LNWR steam locomotive cab, he had to remember that the regulator worked in the opposite direction. Many forgot, and locomotives ended up being reversed through the shed wall of a roundhouse.

▲ When she first appeared, *Turbomotive* must have seemed to be the way ahead, using steam turbines instead of pistons, but she required much attention and, although she survived into the 1950s, she was not a great success. (HMRS)

▲ Another attempt to obtain more power was the 'decapod', the only 0-10-0 locomotive, built as the Lickey banker, but she did at least provide long service. The irony was that she was a Midland locomotive, and the Midland was renowned for its small locomotives! (HMRS)

▲ As nationalisation approached, the railways were recovering from the unavoidable neglect of the war years, as this LMS 2-6-4T with a suburban train leaving Glasgow Central shows. Many of the new British Railways standard locomotives were to be based on Stanier's work for the LMS. (HMRS)

left for government work during the war, first C. Fairburn and then H.G. Ivatt set out to reduce maintenance with improvements to fireboxes and self-cleaning smokeboxes which expelled smaller particles of ash and partly burnt coal through the chimney. Running plates were raised clear of the wheels to improve accessibility.

On the LMS, under Stanier, a locomotive rationalisation and building programme

◀ The standard express locomotive for the new British Railways was the Britannia class, named after distinguished Britons, in this case *Oliver Cromwell*. Many of the Bulleid Pacifics were rebuilt and had a passing resemblance to the Britannia class.

them a distinctive appearance. According to some, the Coronation class with its heavy cladding, largely for publicity purposes, was not pleasing to Stanier, and most of the class, the Dukes and Duchesses as they became known, were without this; it was later removed from the Coronation class, largely to ease maintenance. After Stanier

◀ The way it ended in 1960, with steam having less than ten years left on British Railways. This was *Evening Star*, the last steam locomotive to be built for British Railways, at Swindon. Although intended to be a freight locomotive, she was able to pull passenger trains and in preservation has delighted many enthusiasts over the years.

DAILY SKETCH

FIRE THREATENS A ROYAL HOME

No. 8,787   WEDNESDAY, JUNE 30, 1937   ONE PENNY

Left Euston at 9.50 a.m.

114 M.P.H. BY RAIL!

BRITISH RECORD

Arrived at Crewe (158.1 Miles) at 11.59¾ a.m.   **Left Crewe At 1.55 p.m.**   **Arrived at Euston at 3.54 p.m.**

WIRELESS ON PAGE 16   INSIDE INFORMATION: Weather 3, Spinsters' Letters 6, Candidus 8, Wonderful London 10 and 11, New Serial 19, Children's Page 20, Gertrude Lawrence 21, 'Heavens Are Telling You' 22

◀ A good idea of what the great steam expresses meant to the public was the front-page treatment given to a record-breaking run, as this *Daily Sketch* front page clearly shows.

Did you know?

Much confusion has arisen from the LMS having a class of locomotives known as the Royal Scot class, with the first locomotive actually named *Royal Scot*, and an express train of the same name. Meanwhile, the LNER had a locomotive named the *Flying Scotsman* and, of course, a train of the same name. The LNER, in fact, went a step further with an express freight service known as the 'Green Arrow', and a locomotive with the same name.

saw the number of classes fall from 404 in 1932 to 132 by 1938, while the number of locomotives needed to operate the system fell by 26 per cent.

On the LNER, much work had to await the passing of Sir Nigel Gresley and his successors, Edward Thompson and Arthur Peppercorn, who did much to standardise components and also switch to simpler valve gear that was less temperamental and needed less maintenance.

During the Second World War, the Ministry of Supply and the Ministry of War Transport attempted to enforce greater standardisation of locomotives, favouring Stanier's LMS 2-8-0 design. This rule was often ignored, with Bulleid on the Southern Railway maintaining that his 4-6-2 Merchant Navy class, and the similar West Country and Battle of Britain classes with their lower axle weights, were actually mixed-traffic locomotives. He also produced his own utility design: the Q1 class – a 0-6-0 tender locomotive.

The real drive towards standardisation came with nationalisation. As in the past, there was a locomotive exchange in 1948, but this time the big difference was that the locomotives of all four grouped companies took part, rather than a simple exchange between two companies. The main classes

Did you know?
The famous GWR express, the 'Cheltenham Flyer', only ran at high speed in the 'up' direction; that is, towards London.

all had their strengths and their weaknesses, and the idea was that the best features of each should provide the basis of a new series of standard steam locomotives which would be deployed throughout the regions of the new British Railways.

A number of inherited modern designs were rebuilt to overcome their weaknesses, with the most controversial being the work on Bulleid's 'Spam Cans', which led to his departure from British Railways.

British Railways decided to build nine classes of steam locomotive, all with two cylinders to avoid the problems of internal cylinders. The best features were adopted from the old companies, but route availability was wider than in the past. The 4-6-0 tender locomotives and 2-6-4 tank engines looked much like updated Stanier designs, but the most distinctive locomotive was the Class 9 2-10-0 freight locomotives, which were not only more powerful than the 2-8-0s favoured by the LMS and LNER, but could work fast passenger trains. One of these, *Evening Star*, was the last steam locomotive to be built for British Railways when steam locomotive production ended in 1960.

1804 Penydarren tramroad at Merthyr Tydfil conducts successful experiment with Trevithick locomotive.

1811 John Blenkinsop lays a rack rail line from Middleton Colliery to Leeds, and uses a locomotive built to a modification of the Trevithick design.

1814 Killingworth Colliery wagonway uses George Stephenson's first locomotive *Blucher*.

1825 Official opening of S&DR sees use of Stephenson's *Locomotion*, but while used at the opening for passenger and freight work, initially on normal service steam was solely for freight trains.

1829 Rainhill Trials to find the most suitable locomotive for the LMR.

1830 LMR opens and is the first to use steam locomotives for all traffic.

1841 Robert Stephenson invents link motion valve gear, increasing the effort that could be extracted from a given volume of steam.

1842 Simple form of superheating applied by Hawthorn.

1843 Grand Junction Railway opens Crewe works.

1844   In Belgium, Egide Walschaert invents single eccentric drive valve gear.

1850   Compounding of locomotive cylinders invented by J. Nicholson. Trials held on Eastern Counties Railway.

1859   In France, Henri Giffard invents steam injector allowing water to be fed into boilers while the locomotive is standing still.

***c.*1860**   Charles Markham, Midland Railway, invents modified firebox so that coal can be burned instead of coke as previously.

1860   LNWR installs water pick-up apparatus, invented by John Ramsbottom. Locomotives can now replenish their water tanks without stopping.

1863   Steam locomotives introduced on Festiniog Railway – the world's first narrow-gauge railway when opened in 1836.

1876   In France, Anatole Mallet produces first compound steam locomotive.

1882   F.W. Webb builds first three-cylinder 2-2-2-2 uncoupled compound for the LNWR.

1886   Steam sanding apparatus introduced.

1888   First race to the north with West Coast trains running from Euston to Edinburgh Princes Street and East Coast trains running from King's Cross to Edinburgh Waverley.

1895   Second race to the north with overnight sleeper services from Euston and King's Cross to Aberdeen. West Coast wins.

1897   Four-cylinder 'simplex' 4-4-0s appear.

1898   In Germany, smoke-tube superheater invented by Schmidt.

1904   GWR 'Ocean Mail' from Plymouth to London via Bristol sees the *City of Truro* break the 100mph barrier for the first time between Plymouth and Bristol, but the achievement is unofficial.
GWR commences non-stop running between London Paddington and Plymouth.

*c.***1904** First locomotive testing plant in UK built at Swindon works.

1906 GWR introduces audible cab signalling on the Henley and Fairford branches.

Schmidt superheater introduced to the UK, initially on two Lancashire & Yorkshire Railway locomotives.

Four-cylinder compound Star-class 4-6-0 locomotives appear on GWR.

1908 First British 4-6-2 or Pacific locomotive completed by Churchward for the GWR, but rebuilt as a Castle class in 1924.

1922 Gresley introduces his first Pacific locomotives for the GNR.

1923 GWR introduces the train popularly known as the 'Cheltenham Flyer'.

1925 GWR and LNER conduct locomotive exchange trials, with the GWR locomotives proving to be the more economical.

1927 Non-stop railway services introduced by the LNER between King's

Cross and Newcastle, the world's longest non-stop service at the time.

1928   Non-stop services introduced by the LNER between London King's Cross and Edinburgh Waverley, the world's longest non-stop service at the time.

1929   In France, Andre Chapelon shows that efficiency can be increased by 40 per cent through reducing pressure losses in steam pipes and steam chests, and eventually leads to his Kylchap exhaust system.

1932   The 'Cheltenham Flyer' becomes the world's fastest train with an average speed between Swindon and Paddington of 71.4mph. Later, *Tregenna Castle* achieves an average of 81.7mph.

1935   Non-stop services start with LNER 'Silver Jubilee' streamlined express between London King's Cross and Newcastle, the UK's first streamlined train.

1936   LMS *Princess Elizabeth* runs from Glasgow to London at an average speed of 70mph.

1937   LMS 'Coronation Scot' streamlined express commences between London Euston and Glasgow Central. On trials, 114mph is attained approaching Crewe.

1938   LNER A4 Pacific *Mallard* sets a world speed record for steam locomotives of 126mph.

1948   After nationalisation of Great Britain's railways, locomotives are exchanged between former company areas to identify the basis for a standard design.

1951   First of nine British Railways standard steam locomotive classes appears.

1958   Last steam locomotive to be built at Crewe works.

1960   Last steam locomotive to be built for British Railways, *Evening Star*, outshopped at Swindon.

BOOKS

Ellis, Chris, and Morse, Greg, *Steaming Through Britain*, NRM/
    Conway, 2010.
Nock, O.S., *The Railway Enthusiast's Encyclopaedia*, Hutchinson,
    1968.
Simmons, Jack, and Biddle, Gordon, *The Oxford Companion to
    British Railway History*, OUP, 2000.
Wragg, David, *A Historical Dictionary of the Railways of the British
    Isles*, Wharncliffe, 2009.

WEBSITES

Historic Model Railway Society (HMRS), www.hmrs.org.uk
National Railway Museum, www.nrm.org.uk
Railway Correspondence and Travel Society, www.rcts.org.uk
Science Museum, www.sciencemuseum.org.uk

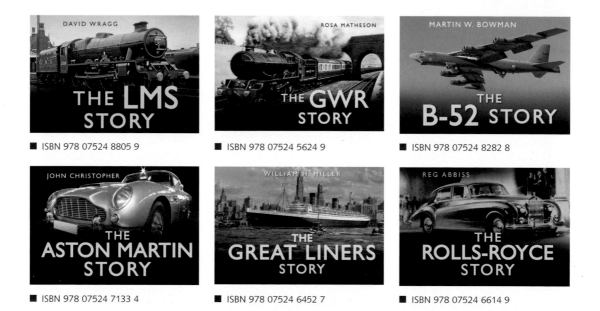